This book is dedicated to:

My three sons, Kurt, Jamie, Leo
For who I still breathe and have never ending love.

For my family (to name you all would be a book in itself) and my Mam who passed away in February 2018.
My stepdad Gordon who gave my Mam 39 years of life and the love she truly deserved.

James and Sue, for their unwavering friendship and support with all things connected to Rusty Goat's Poetry Corner, and the friends who have stuck by me through the darkest hours of my life.

The mental health and wellbeing being charities; Twigs Community Garden Project and IPSUM who have helped me rebuild and gain confidence to grow.

And for those not mentioned by name, you know who you are.

First published in the United Kingdom in 2019.
© Scott Cowley and Scott Cowley Not Under My Breath 2019

Scott Cowley has asserted his right under the Copyright, Designs and Patents Act, 1988 to be identified as the author of this work

All rights reserved. This book or any portion thereof may not be reproduced or used in any manner whatsoever without the express written permission of the publisher except for the use of brief quotations in a book review.
First published in the United Kingdom in 2019
by Bite Poetry Press.
www.bitepress.co.uk

ISBN 978-1-913218-28-7

First Edition

Cover photography and design by Gerard Hughes
www.gerardhughes.co.uk

Printed and bound in the UK by Biddles, Castle House East Winch Road, King's Lynn PE32 1SF

NOT UNDER MY BREATH

SCOTT COWLEY

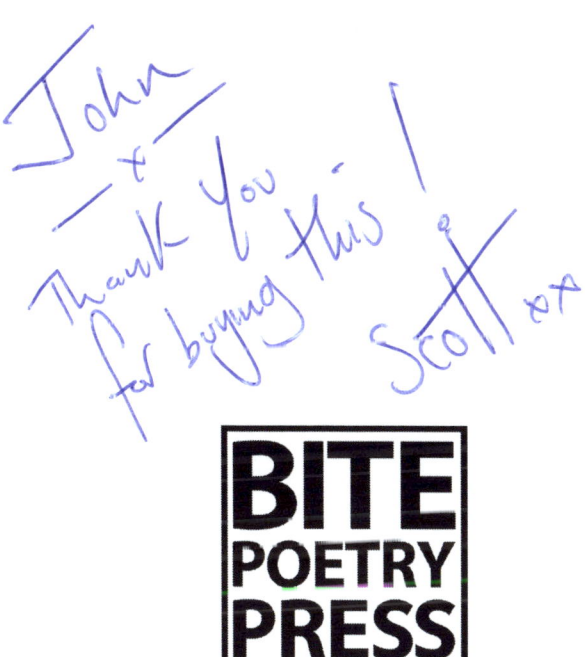

Contents

9	CRISIS	
11		Crisis And Discovery
12		It Just Is
13		A Harsh Wind
14		Darkest Hours
16		Distorted Dark Hours
18		The Stench Of Cheap Bleach
10		Crisis And Discovery
21	DISCOVERY	
22		Not Under My Breath
26		Stones And Sticks
30		Just One More Step
32		I Have To Lay In It
36		How Did You Sleep?
37		How Hard Can It Be?
38		A Thousand Miles From Sainthood
40		November Sun
42		365 Days
45	NAMELESS AND UNSEEN	
47		Four-Forty-Four
48		Ten-Fifty-Seven
50		Views Of Four Streets
53		Bazooka Terry
54		Nameless And Unseen
56		From Darkness To Light

59	BLACK HEARTS AND CROOKED CARDS
60	Greed And Corruption
62	Know It All
63	Black Hearts And Crooked Cards
64	Nothing Better To Do
65	You'd Be Wrong To Assume
66	Selective Visualisation
68	So You've Got The Measure Of Me?
71	THOUGHTS OF YOU
72	Just A Rainbow Away
74	Thoughts Of You
75	Late Last Night
76	With Each Breath
77	I Call Him Freddy
78	Which Words Did You Write?
81	Sundays With The Boy
82	Our Routine
85	PENCIL MARKS ON PAGES
86	A Tale Or Two
89	I Like It But It's Clunky
90	Pencil Marks On Pages
92	Self Educated Ramblings
94	I Wonder
96	Wicker Not Wood

Author's Note

Thank you for choosing to buy this book, my first collection of spoken word poetry.
These pieces have been written over the last two or three years, and are a reflection of some very dark times, loss, battling with sobriety and a lifelong struggle with Borderline Personality Disorder, and anger directed at social injustices, but also focus on love and recovery.
On the whole, offering a reflective and inspiring collection of poetry.

Opening doors for conversation into difficult subjects.

Scott Cowley

CRISIS

Crisis And Discovery

Crisis and recovery
A journey of deep soul searching discovery
Don't smother don't cover me
This is my time you'll get over me

Lost in time, all hovery
Sat on cliff edge, don't bother me
136 to try and smother me
Here and now simplicity
This name, this name you gave to me
Who am I, who am I to be?
Can't sleep for nights
Smoke, drink a brew with me
Is this how it's supposed to be?

Step follows step
Deliberate not expertly
You've asked who
Who gave these words to me
You put a mic
A mic in front of me
Is this how it ought to be?

You'll find peace
Where your peace will be
This is now
A time for me to be
I'm no preacher
No god to be

This is
My crisis
My recovery
My journey
My discovery

It Just Is

It is a gift as it is a curse
It is emptiness and joy

It is cold and a warm embrace
It is something and yet nothing

It wasn't by choice, neither do I now ignore it
It is the sweet smell of roses and their thorns

It just is

A Harsh Wind

Been lying here awake for what feels like forever
My mind has wandered far and deep
As it normally does when I cannot sleep
Conjuring up images of past times at 03:27

I close my eyes and count backwards from 99
My chosen routine on many occasion
This is my eleventh repeated attempt
A cycle which appears to never end at 03:27

I lay in my bed eyes wide open again
A harsh wind blows leaves through deserted quiet streets
Apart from this noise it appears silent outside
The tick of the clock appears to have stopped at 03:27

I appear to be drifting my consciousness shifting
That comfortable warm sinking shrinking feeling
I can feel myself slipping and sleep awaits me
Praying for dreams to take me far from here at 03:27

My mind is in knots contorted and fucked
The quilt is twisted wrapped around me constricted
Inside my mind screaming please take away these demons
I am not ready for nightmares to take me at 03:27

The peace that I prayed for is just beyond a locked door
A night of restful sleep is still just out of reach
I'd give my soul for that key to release me
And let me drift into deep sweet sleep at 03:27

Darkest Hours

Three-Oh-Six AM and I find myself
In this dark cold emptiness
Where not even a mouse is stirring
Let alone awake

All I can hear is
The rapidly increasing
Beat of my heart
My thoughts flit and skip
And the piercing silence
Of the darkness overrides

My fragile mind it dripfeeds me
What I know to be are lies
Those questions, no those statements
That are so loud at this time of night
Chipping away one tick of the clock at a time
Each tock as loud as the hours chime

I writhe restless my body soaked in sweat
From my stone cold feet to
What little hair I have on my head
My eyes open filled with the blackest of light
Which takes hold at the darkest hours of night

Memories hitting me full on
Point blank two shotgun cartridges
Are emptied into my chest
My skin torn to shreds
My heart ripped to pieces
And I'm left, I'm left wrestling
Long lost last chances and regrets

I writhe restless
My stone cold feet
Eyes filled with black light
Body soaked in sweat

I find myself naked
Naked as the day I was born
Bathed in the bright white
Stark harshness of the bathroom light
The mirror reflecting a face
The image of which I often hate
And this time I do not hesitate

Long lost last chances
Two shotgun cartridges
Memories hitting full on
Heart ripped to pieces

The stark harshness
Naked as day born
Mirror reflecting
And I do not hesitate

This time I do not hesitate

I take a cut throat razor to my neck

Because it's true
To kill the beast

You have to first remove its head

Distorted Dark Corners

Another festive period is upon me
The battle to avoid demons taunt me
Memories haunt me endlessly
Beating repeatedly seeking me

Seasonal street light displays glow softly
Illuminating the footpaths where I walk
Yesterday's light shines bright behind me
Casting shadows from the past on walls

Dark shapes of lost hope
Dark shapes of twisted faces
Dark shapes of bitter taste
Dark shapes of lost love

Memories which haunt me
Twist and contort me
Shadows in the lonely
Distorted dark corners of my mind

In a click of fingers
By smells I'm transported
Distorting the fucked up state
Of my twisted sense of reality

I stand elbow resting on the bar
Sipping iced water from a glass
The thick sickly sweet smell
Of Southern Comfort In the glass next to me
Brings twisted flashbacks
Thrashing crashing horrendously

I lived in shadows
In unnamed dark seedy bars

Face shaded
Using the dark light of night
To hide my face and
The shame of a wasted life

Still twisted and affected by this for days
I retreat to the safety behind my locked front door
You see all this is very draining on my sanity
Episodes like this can set me back weeks

And then there's the flip
Me stood here doing this
Baring my soul
Open honest hard hitting lines

I often ask myself why
What do I do this for?

I'm compelled propelled
By some sort of invisible force
I'm no preacher but I have a need
And maybe it's redemption I seek?

I'll continue to tell tales of being torn
Dark corners from where verse is born

I'll know when it's time
To change tracks

Until then, well
You know the formula

The Stench Of Cheap Bleach

I am an unfinished symphony
Do not write me off just yet
Do not dismiss me

I began to see
A little more clearly
Relatively recently I admit

Through the thickest of fogs
Tired miles I have trod repeatedly
Unsteadily beating back
The chains of ill health
That tried to swallow me

At times when I'd thought life
Had beaten me
Sectioned for my own safety

Knife edge
Cliff edge
Drunk isolation
Hospital bed

Those stark white walls
Cygnet ward corridors

The stench
Of cheap bleach
The grinding of
My teeth

The too often heard
Panic button siren
Which rattled off
Those tortured walls

To return to this prison
I know is not my decision

For a click of fingers
Is all it takes
To re-loop that noose
Hanging from loft hatch

Well here's today's truth
The chair from under loft hatch
I have removed
The same chair which once
Held me so steadily

For now
I still breathe

Do not
Write me off
Just yet

For I am
The unfinished
Symphony

DISCOVERY

Not Under My Breath

My sobriety is being tested
Demons of alcohol are pestering me
Confronted by another period of being tormented
And my drinking arm is becoming restless

The demons see my weakening state
That pint of ale in handled glass I can taste
It's not that I've won but each day is another I'm winning
I've come too far to be crushed by giving in

My ability to resist is thinning
Two pints please landlord of Sharp's Brewery's finest
No problem he replies with a wry smile
He cares not for my weakness

Ten pounds deliberately vigorously slapped on the bar
That first pint does not even wet my lips
I look skywards ignoring the inner voice, my choice
Without second thought I grip the next in my fist

Fuck sobriety
Fuck resistance
Fuck it all
Fuck it all for an instance

I've given in to resistance sobriety broken
I shudder at the taste of hops malt and water
The Devil's daughters
That old friend I knew so well returns
And I say under my breath, I have missed you

It begins to twist and contort me
Slowly slowly I detach from reality
The steps I'd made to a life of normality

Lay shattered and strewn besides me
I pay little heed to the shouts inside my mind
As the positive pieces I'd been putting together
Lay scattered
This night will end with me bruised battered and scarred
Set em' up landlord and I'll knock the shots over
One after another

The bar is crowded rowdy too fucking loud for me
I stumble and trip as I stagger towards putrid urinals
Fumbling for my zip at a trough of stinking piss
Propped up against the wall nauseous I vomit

Head spinning through memories tormented
The innocence of my children's faces their smiles
Now replaced by horror, tears streaming

The months I'd spent repairing bridges
Digging myself out of bottomless ditches
Stitching up the invisible scars
Piecing back together broken hearts
In a blink of an eye have vanished

In the gutter broken again
In the gutter alone without friends
With little memory
With pockets empty
I slip towards hell for eternity

I awake from this nightmare so vivid
Livid inside with my life that once was
The sweat on my skin that I woke with
A harsh frost that I'll take as a warning

I sit and drink coffee
Slowly coming round to reality
Thankful for this life laid before me
And the lessons it's taught me

I close my eyes
See their faces
And I say this time
Not under my breath

I promise you boys
I will not waste this

"Piecing back together broken hearts..."

Stones And Sticks

Stones and sticks have the ability
To inflict cuts bruises disability
Words will never hurt we
Who was the wanker first said that?
Where the fuck was their head at?

Been fighting since before I could run
Ripped to shreds
Heart weeping
Eyes bleeding
Crucified mentally
Literally year after year
Decades four

A journey now just begun
I ain't stepped up unable
Unable to continue
No laying down
Playing deaf
Playing dumb
Believe this is heartfelt
Time on my hands
Hatching plans

I was sat on a cliff edge
And said don't bother me
An off duty police officer spotted me
And I was pulled back from
Pulled back from a place
Of fucking with fate

A fresh diagnosis
From a doctor of psychology
Hammer hit nail square
BPD
PTSD
Traits of Bipolar
The only letters that'll follow my name

I'll not sit silently boxed
Realistically not expecting to be
Part of folklore history
It'll be more like a hit or a mystery

All I did was pull out the choke
And turn ignition with key

Education education education
Was not my vocation
That horse bolted
Long before I'd got sight of it
Jumped five bar gate
Tapped out steel shoon beat across cattle grate
Like Ginger and Fred
On Broadway boards

Ginger hair receded
Receded beyond existence
Life disappearing into the distance
It's no dressed up rehearsal
And it's never too late
Never too late to rebuild a life
And make the last third count

I'll throw no punches visibly
You'll not see physicality
But be told
These words come from soul deep
And I've never harvested
What ain't worthy to keep

I'm a father foremostly
I'm a friend stoically
I'm a brother the younger
I'm a son of my mother
I'm a son of Freddy
Believe me when I say
Never again I'll mention he

Not over verbosely able I'll admit
Natural born ability questionable?
But strip it back to the bone
Boil it right down
It's Rusty Goat Poetry...
And the wizardry
Of spoken word delivery

"Muscle tearing vomitless retching"

Just One More Step

I've fallen again
And I've got no energy
To keep fighting it
To keep fighting with it

Each breath
Every step

That follows breath
That follows step
That follows
That follows
That follows

Each step
Every breath

And then I'm running with it
One drink won't kill
I stumble but never spill a drop
Well practiced at these antics
Taking it too far once too often
Renowned for my inability to say no
I'd go wherever the drink was dripping
The only thing about what I was thinking

Pass me the fucking bottle
And I'll throttle all life out of it
Until I'm passed out with it
Clutching it like a security blanket
A fragile glass comfort zone
A comfortably numb warm embrace

If only I knew back then
With hindsight
If I only knew
If I only understood my mind

Post drink induced depression
Bouts of alcoholic psychosis
Drunk without inhibition
Not to mention the use of
Psychoactive recreational substances
Euphoria followed by paranoia
Hazy next day vague memories
Stomach churning anxiety
Muscle tearing vomitless retching
Followed by deep dark hollow
Isolation and the emptiness
The unbearable emptiness

And true to form
I return again
To a trusted
Reliable close friend

I twist the cap
I open up the wrap
I slip slowly
I feel alive again

Each breath
Every step

That follows breath
That follows step
That follows
That follows
That follows

Each step
Every breath

Closer to the edge
Just one more step

I Have To Lay In It

Laying in my pit has never been productive
But it stops me being externally destructive

A temporary impenetrable shelter
Covers pulled over
Covered up
But under, it's the gates of hell

Demons tormenting
Relentless
Fingernails scraping inside
Unforgiving

In my mind hosting act after act
Replaying the past
One fucked up fact after fact
Questioning the way I did act

A messed up bundle of bones
Wrapped up in a paper thin bag of skin
An alcoholic substance abuser
No question about it, a fucking loser

Eyes hopeless unable to focus
Rattling around full of valium and codeine
Dysfunctional and chaotic
A lifetime of crisis

No concern about the effects my actions
Would have on those around me
No concern about the direction
Or where my actions would take me
Not wanting to focus on those close to me
Those that cared and held nothing but love for me
Steered by a need to destroy love

Before love had the opportunity to turn
Snap back react and bite me

Fully prepared to destroy myself
How fucking low could one man sink?
A deliberate unjustifiable selfish act
On a belly full of drink I took an overdose
In front of the woman that loved me

Three days later I was back on the drink

A desperate fucked up loser
Alcoholic substance abuser

And the woman
The woman who loved me
The pain I put her through
The mother of our son
The woman who picked me up
Physically and emotionally
The woman who continually supported me

She stayed by my side
Time after time

By my side during those 48 hours
Holding my hand while I laid in that bed
Full of tubes
Poised between life and death
Full of tubes
Poised between heaven and hell
And I expected her forgiveness

She stayed by my side
Time after time

They say sharing can be cathartic
Maybe this time
I've stepped beyond the line
Revealed too much?

Should I have kept this confined
Within the safety of four walls
White sticker club
Group therapy

Have I gone beyond the bounds?
Travelled too far into uncharted territory?
Beyond the bounds
The bounds of poetic decency?

Me, I made the decisions
Me, I destroyed the love
Me, I ignored the caring loving voices
Me, I the self destructive

I'm squaring up to my actions
Accepting the punishments laid upon me
I've no more the need to hide under cover
No longer am I sheltering behind others

I've cleared my vision and made decisions
I'm slowly making amends for my past actions

And I live by the words inked upon me

Each day I will get up and make my bed
Because each night it is me who has to lay in it

"The woman who continually supported me"

How Did You Sleep?

So she asked how did you sleep?
So here is my reply, too deep?

I slept like a sword with two sides
Eyes closed but inside awake

Do I get up or lay around in bed?
Bread can't be buttered on both sides
Cake can't be had and eaten
Wishing there was a reset button

Not being able to give a straight answer
A jumble of metaphor inside my head
Washing machine on spin cycle
White turned grey, from a distance it looks OK?

Am I on the right track close to a station
Speaking in tongues, even dining with the same nation?

Dawning of an age, separation from decasion
The crockery sits child, ball in hand to smash

Gift or a curse
Sow's ear silk purse
To have and hold
Gates to unfold

Curtains to be drawn
Book to leave open
Brakes to apply
Wheels set in motion

Explanation desperation
Delusional hallucination
Steadfast outlast
Full stop

How Hard Can It Be?

Medication induced sleep
Brings a temporary relief
A coma like state
Where my mind takes a break

When I wake
Still in a tormented state
My mind does not have the ability
To decipher dreams from reality

Get a grip and pull yourself together
Have THEY ever felt like this?

How hard can it be'?
We all have DAYS LIKE THESE
But have you ever had weeks
Where days like these
Are all stitched together?

Weathering this out once more
My mind is tattered
Haggard and torn
Forlorn once more and crushed

To the outside world
My actions may appear deliberate
Deconstructive, inconsiderate

When just an hour ago
I could've stood tall, with
The ability to conquer all

But I'm reduced again
To a curled up ball

Medication
Induced sleep
Brings a
Temporary relief

A Thousand Miles From Sainthood

I used to live the high life and dine out most nights on
Cocktails of prescription medication, weed and amphetamines
With the odd cheeky line of the unpurest shit from Peru
All washed down
With Jim Beam, Canadian Club and Wild Turkey 101

Recreational drug experimentation
Wasn't taught in school officially
Skinning up with Soap Bar at lunchtime like it was cool
It was self education of adolescence
Maybe I should have taken up chemistry
Instead of passing out on trichloroethane
Sat at the back in double history

As bad as this was
The ironic twist is
I was pretty damn good
At doing all this

I'll never drink tango again it will forever be tainted
With the taste of bargain basement own brand vodka
Flashbacks to that morning
Sat in cold bath with bottle empty
Blade in hand searching with cuts for the femoral artery

I patched myself up packed a bag and fucked off
Bought a deliberately one way ticket to Manchester Piccadilly
Sobered up, the police picked me up
And yeah Joanne you saved me

As bad as this was
The ironic twist is
I was pretty damn good
At doing all this
Yeah I admit I probably smoke too much

This beats the shit out of toking too much
And the horrendous drug induced psychosis
That went hand in hand with that habit

The battles inside my head with the imagined enemies
Brought on by smoking what you call high grade
Well back in the day we smoked Temple Ball and Sensi
Rolled in green Rizla
Licking the seam of a Number One Embassy

And I wonder sometimes
Too much I admit
Why my head
Is as fucked up as it is?

I choose to avoid intoxicants wherever possible
The spirits remain seal safely intact on the shelf
Maybe I'll fall just like the best have at times
I guess I'll never wander too far from the bottle

In a few years maybe I'll have things in order
When I've got a firm grip of the BPD chaos and disorder
Until then I'll live with acceptance and learned lessons

And I wonder sometimes
Too much I admit to this
What life would have been
Without questionable choices?

I've done more wrong than I'll ever do good
And I'm a thousand miles from sainthood

But...
I'm patching up scars and repairing broken hearts
And dealing with my demons through wordcraft

November Sun

It's cold as I step outside
The low November sun hurts my eyes
These sunglasses I wear
Are not a just a practical thing
They stop the outside world from looking in

My eyes are tired
The whites are cracked
By the tormented hours
Of long sleepless nights

The highs have gone they never last
And I'm returning again to the past

All the medication, those pills
Only serve to keep out the chill

My eyes are shaded
Soul tired restless
Face expressionless
A stone faced defense

Yes I've made mistakes
Haven't we all?
Yes I've burned bridges
And locked firmly closed doors

I take one step forward
Stumble back three
This body is willing
My mind won't release me

All the medication those pills
Only serve to keep out the chill

I'm doing my best and keeping off the drink
I've washed the destructive pills down the sink

It'll take time to get life back on line
But I'm ready to detangle the string

365 Days

Not that long ago I was in the bottom of a pit
As a rough calculation it's been 52 weeks
I have to admit life had never been so shit
And they say all things happen for a reason

A homeless shelter was my temporary address
My state of mental health was in crisis
Decisions were often being made for me
At times completely detached from reality

All the while the world was happening around me
It was almost impossible to accept the facts
Unable to look at my own reflection
My vulnerability stood out lit up by neon lights

I had to put trust in those around me
Those that provided care and support
Family friends and health professionals
The strangers who held out their hands

Strangers who crossed to the same side of the street
Held out their hands and warmly greeted me
These genuine gestures of generosity
Were completely alien
After a lifetime of using isolation for my own protection

Pointed and steered in different directions
Minutes turned to hours and days did unfold
Putting trust in the friendships I was building around me
Beginning to see that the world was not my enemy

I took control took hold and began to address
And suppress the devils and demons inside
The realisation was a moment of awakening
That the rest of this life is down to me

Well here I am, and here I stand
I've weathered four consecutive seasons
That's 365 days as a rough calculation
And still they say all things happen for a reason

Decisions being made for me
Completely detached from reality
Had to watch had to sit back
Until I got my life back on track

My fear of rejection needed protection
With a new tack came my resurrection
I picked up the mic and began to ramble
And you'll have to turn the amp off to stop me

And maybe just maybe
They are right in what they say
That all things
All things happen for a reason

NAMELESS AND UNSEEN

Four-Forty-Four

Blowing cigarette smoke through the light
Of the desk lamp at four-forty-four
It turns out that sleep
Doesn't come visiting here no more

The clock ticks as I sit here alone
In the light from the lamp
I grip pencil in hand
And scratch strings of syllables
Across pressed pulp

The early shifters begin to go about their business
Flashing amber lights bounce off shop windows
As the commercial refuse collectors go about emptying
Wheeled skips of yesterday's unwantedness

A lone figure crosses from one side of the street to another
The button on the pedestrian crossing goes unpressed
And the night walker disappears out of sight

The light from the estate agents' window display
Shines bright
And I wonder how many houses they have sold at this hour
As the clock ticks Five-Oh-Four

The opposite corner of Bath Road is bathed in darkness
Fronted on two sides by glass panes in blue gloss frames
Is a shoe shop, just a short hop from where I sit
During trading hours I've never seen anyone enter or exit
And I wonder what goes on behind its doors?

Five-Fifteen AM
And the button
On the pedestrian crossing
Remains unpressed

Ten-Fifty-Seven

Midweek revellers walk the beat
And filter their way in small clusters
To the bars on Wood Street

A small group of four exit the tapas bar

A taxi waits on hazard lights
Half parked on the pavement
It appears a few words are exchanged
Between one of the four and driver
Through the nearside passenger front window
They open three of the four doors and enter

Hazard lights are turned off
They head off in the taxi
Direction east, roughly

A couple are stood in the doorway of the estate agents
Illuminated by the display lights
He sparks a cigarette and she peers at house rentals
They embrace, her arm around his waist
And from their movements I sense there is laughter

The relative silence is broken by sirens
Two cars pull to the kerb, an ambulance comes into view
It's obviously been heard and observed which pleases me
It passes with ease and makes its way
To the blues and twos destination

Cars pass in ones and twos, I wouldn't say it's busy
But these movements will continue almost endlessly
Through night and day with varying frequency

A lone figure staggers
The effects of one too many
Even on a Wednesday night
Hands will clutching a head, unsoothable
Tomorrow morning

I roll another cigarette

A mixed group of six or seven pass in the street below
The air rings with calls and shouts
I smile to myself and remember when that walk was my beat

Ten-Fifty-Seven PM
I sit back
Retract the point of my pen
With a thumb press

Views Of Four Streets

The number 11 bus rounds the corner
As I sit here drinking coffee
On this blustery November morning

A delivery is made, my guess is it's cakes
For consumption with coffee, probably
I pull the sleeves down on my hoody
Push my thumbs through the holes in the cuffs
Which have been designed for this purpose

The view of four streets becomes busier
As the time on the clock on the inside
Of the coffee shop door nears Nine-Thirty
My drink cools quickly
On this cold November morning
And I take sips more frequently

The pedestrian crossing lights are flashing amber
A driving instructors car stalls as it pulls away
Inside the car I imagine there is a certain level of panic
This situation will be dealt with by the instructor
In a calm and professional manner

A car behind sounds it's horn impatiently
The driver obviously frustrated by the situation
I guess the driver is forgetful
Of the time when they were a learner

The instructors car engine starts
It begins to pull away
With more engine revs than necessary
But, still smoothly

My mind wanders
On this cold early Winter's morning
And brings up memories of a family holiday
I once took in Cyprus
It was some five years ago now
In the March of Twenty-Thirteen

I remember many things about that holiday
The warm sun, the friendly local people
And the time when I were a family man

Life has changed a lot since then
And the memories are fond ones

I finish my coffee, pull the hood over my head
And walk the short distance to the bus stop
To catch the number eleven into town

"I grip pencil in hand"

Bazooka Terry

Behind the bike shed she kissed a boy called Terry
The sweet funny guy she sat next to in biology
It turns out second period was double chemistry!
Chemistry and smiles from kissing with Terry

Her best friend Susan dated Frank
Frank was Terry's big brother
He was a discerning stylish character
Frank had a white Vauxhall Viva

Terry's ride was more in line with their teenage crush
Two up on his Raleigh racer
With the handlebars turned up down Kings Hill
You couldn't see them for dust wind gust

They rode up around town without disaster
Terry knew all along what this girl was after
The air would be sweetened with more than laughter
The taste on his lips is what she was after

After that fantastic first date ride
Once she'd cleared the tears from her eyes
A wind whipped infliction from Terry's rather long black and yellow school tie
She knew this long haired lover of football was her guy to be

A guy she could refer to as us as in we
A guy to take round her Nan's for tea

Terry tasted of Bazooka bubble gum
Sweetly

Nameless And Unseen

The homeless man
Asks passersby for change again
'Scuse me guv
Can you spare a pound?

Through the streets
Lost alone cold and dirty
Scraping the floor for discarded cigarette butts
Praying for a change of luck

Turned away from the shelter
Sorry John, no beds tonight
For countless months this has been
His nightly routine
Wandering the streets
Nameless and unseen

He carries his life in two plastic bags
Thrown over his shoulder is a quilt
Dirty damp and stained
Tonight this will be his bed again

He scraped through skips
For cardboard boxes to make a mattress
To help keep the cold
From chilling him to the bone
Praying he's not moved on
From the high street doorway

Through restaurant windows
Watching people eat
He does not make it obvious
Their tables over laden with food
Oblivious to his daily struggle
Have they ever known real hunger?

A change of approach
He tries to start a conversation
Praying the next person who stops
Makes eye contact for a brief moment
And sees him as a human
Not just another homeless

A woman stops
And asks his name
He says it's John

She reaches for her purse
And hands him three pound coins
This will buy him tea and soup
From the all night café by the station

As this nameless woman wanders on her way
She wonders where did it all go wrong
For that homeless man?
The man she now knows as John

Will he make it through another
Cold winter night?
Sometimes he prays not to wake
From his tormented sleep
Praying that this night
Will bring the sleep of endless dreams

But John wakes again
Chilled to the bone
Confronted by another day
And the endless cycle continues

'Scuse me guv
Can you spare a pound?

From Darkness To Light

Pulls on a new pair of kicks
Looks in the mirror and tips himself a wink
Pulls open the front door unlocked
Looks down at his watchless wrist
Gives a wry smile at what he thinks
The fact time means little to nothing

With fight inside he strides
The days no longer dark as night
With fight inside he strides
With days he's turned from dark to light

He's been battered
With a crippling affliction
He's been beaten
With days as black as nights

The fact of matter he's risen from beaten
The fact of the matter he shrugged off battered

His mind was tattered
His bones did clatter

Through gritted teeth stained chipped
Striving forward determined yet haggard

Waist deep through disconnected disassociation
Through unjust decisions and justifications
Breaking through from the outside
Breaking through with head held high

He strides
Dark as night
With fight
Dark to light

"Have they ever known real hunger?"

BLACK HEARTS AND CROOKED CARDS

Greed And Corruption

Fuck this system which breeds
Dishonesty, disease, greed and corruption
Bankers, politicians and multinationals
With their shady deals, backhanders
And unjustifiable sky high bonus system
With clever manipulation of the press
And media system
All within minutes is seemingly forgotten

A high street filled with coffee shops
Who suck the money from your pockets
And give back very little in taxes
Nothing we can do say they say
It's loopholes in a system
The same system designed by
The same thieving, lying, scheming
Corrupt politicians

Those with disabilities stripped of their benefits
And forced to line up at food banks to feed
Taxes pulled out of thin air
If you've more rooms than you need
And the honest working man
Has his pockets ransacked time and time again
While politicians line their already bursting purses

Front line services
Including doctors and nurses
Facing pitiful pay rises

A NHS system run on guilt
The guilt of those who chose
To dedicate their lives to saving souls

And an education system
More concerned with league table results

Than actually producing what this country needs
Which is individuals with their own minds
And their own voices
Instead of being taught how to think
Before you've even finished suckling on milk

Dumb down the population
With mindless fucking television
Commercials to convince you
That the latest car and the biggest TV
Will make you happy
Distracted from what's really going on
Poverty on every street
A country on its fucking knees

Billions spent waging wars in foreign lands
Fighting extremists armed with the weapons
That the so called civilised western world sold them
And we hear of young men and women
Being radicalised time and time again
A backwash of racial hatred
Fighting on our own streets
All in the name of greed

Welcome to the world of greed and corruption
Where all your ill dealings are forgiven
If you've got the pounds to line the pockets
Of the morally rotten

But come judgement day
At the top of the steps
Signposted for heaven and hell
The corrupt will be begging
Asking for forgiveness
Retracting their words
Denying their dishonest actions.
Shut the gates, let them feel the fucking flames!

Know It All

When you sit here alone and it's getting late
And you've realised you don't know it all
You're listening to the words of Mark.e.Smith
Is it too late to get into The Fall!?

Another bottle of brown cap popped open
Your dreams are dreams not reality
It's Monday to Friday in a shop office or factory
Are you happy with that until all the clocks stop?

We are a disease riddled, drug fuelled, binge drinking nation
Selfish at the dawn of the end of creation
I don't know about you but I want to get off
I want to pull the cord before the final stop

We've pumped all the oil and sucked all the gas
We've burned all the coal whilst asleep on the sofa
Watched the TV about the decline of our world
Cracked another beer and uttered a few tuts

You've sat here a written about your disgust
And expressed concern over the inevitable dust
In front of the fire nice TV sofa and all
In the world outside last orders are being called

The question remains the same
And the song unchanged
You've realised you don't know it all

You're listening to the words of Mark.e.Smith
Is it too late to get into The Fall?

Black Heart And Crooked Cards

It's scary to think how quick shit changes
When your ticking along just flicking through life's pages
Remembering places faces and those who for the sake of peace
With their twisted take on reality
Go unnamed behind gritted teeth

It's a crying shame in the age of anti-social media
That all meaning of this phrase has been lost
'In the strictest of confidence between you and me only'
No matter which way you turn you see nobody to trust

That niggling doubt which has cast dark shadows for months
Where you've ignored the gut feeling and hunches
And bent over backwards to please
Has done nothing but germinate that dormant bitter seed

I feel hatred, anger and all flavours of bitter
Ignored my own feelings for the sake of others
Which is a part of me and my kindness for those
Who are not kith or kin but still I call sister or brother

I've seen, I can be settled inside knowing
It's you and not me who has been deceitful behind
I am open and speak without forked tongue
No words I have spoken have been twisted or wrong

I'm done with your putrid sneaky bedevilment
For I have truly seen your scales and snake eyes

Now that I've set this in poetic verse
I'll be able to leave it, but from afar
I shall watch you and see others
Mark your black heart and crooked cards

Nothing Better To Do

Why assume I've got nothing better to do
Just because I don't have a job like you?
Slams diary down with a frown like thunder
Yeah just you wait you'll soon fall too
When that rug is pulled from under you

Step away walk away leave the situation
Is there need for you to feel this way?
A need for a red line reaction
Knowing you're not wrong
Is that not enough satisfaction?

Well that's where you'd be wrong to assume
And then what do you want me to do
Exchange my key for a dessert spoon?

Just because you gave me the key to a room
The right is not handed to you
To treat me the way you see fit to

Dissatisfied with treating me with contempt
You looked bemused when I began to vent
Dissatisfied with that down your nose staring
Like I owe you something after I've paid what's due
Well just you mind me when your foot is in my shoe

You'd Be Wrong To Assume

Under here, yes under your roof
Here I am, yes me living proof no spoof
I am not stone to be picked from horse hoof
I am not neck in noose
Here I am living proof

No stone in hoof, neck in noose
A hand full of change but I'm the full shilling
Yeah very chilling isn't it
But do not be afraid
I am safe where I sit

Hit not miss
Tip-top not crisis
Table for two
Not sniper church tower crisis

No neck
No stone
No hoof
No noose

Living
Breathing
Proof

Selective Visualisation

Endlessly
Playing chess
With texts
Breath wasted

I never tried to twist
You up with metaphor
Needless endless riddles
And your intellect was
Never at question

It's straight to say
Ignorance is never
An attractive trait

Your selective visualisation
Of the questions relevance

Or the simple fact that
Your eyes don't want to hear
The words that you read

"I am not neck in noose"

So You've Got The Measure Of Me?

Take a look at your own reflection
Re-centre your twisted perception
Buy yourself a mirror tell me what you see

So why do you have a problem with me?

Double check the bubble in your
Out of straight moral spirit level
Before making assumptions based on
Your own misguided sense of horizontal

You travel following twisted lines
On a faded water damaged map
Well let me tell you this
Unlike this map the world isn't flat

Navigation with your un-compassed ideology
Pointless single minded sense of moral direction
You'll need more than a key-ringed rabbits foot
So I wish you luck with where you end up with that!

I see things and I'm not talking hallucinations
I've had my ear to the ground for a while now
Witnessed first hand blazing flaming licks of the fire
The smoke signals I've seen with my own eyes

To be honest
With of all this
I'm becoming tired
My patience expired

It's not like I haven't been holding out my hand
Opening doors allowing you to walk through
There are things I fail to get my head around
Why would anyone choose to bite another's hand?

You still think you've got
The measure of me?
Well I suggest you retract
Sit the fuck down and
Double check the facts!

THOUGHTS OF YOU

Just A Rainbow Away

You are just a rainbow away
Not far, just a few steps
Closed eyes, bring us closer

You referred to me as your uncle big brother
And I referred to you as my little sister

The time should have been longer
On that thought I'll not linger
You'd not want there to be bitter
You'd want the memories to be sweet
With just a few memories
Memories I'll forever treasure

The few days we spent together
Those precious moments
The laughter through tears
The laughter through pain
My hours of wishing
Wishing that you'd not suffer
Wanting to shoulder your burden

My heart hurts now
My heart feels pain
My mind knows this will pass
I know you'll forever remain

The pain will ease in time
The love will never leave

I will look up into the night sky
With a tear in my eye
I will keep stepping forward
I'll continue to make you proud

In this life for us left behind
Our hearts still beat
Memories you've left for us to keep
In our mind's eye never forgotten

In our dreams
And our waking hours
Until we meet again
Until the next life

You are
Just a
Rainbow away

Thoughts Of You

In retrospect
With hindsight
I'd not have fallen in love with you
And I'd not be sat here
Smoking cigarettes at three in the morning
Running myself over
Stripping my back bare with birch
Retracing all done
Retracing all said
The support you gave
The support I never sought
Until it was too late

The empty bottles
The sick you mopped up
The man you loved
The wreck that I was

Every time I say goodbye
As I walk away
In pain
With thoughts of you

Late Last Night

I picked up my phone
To call you
Late last night

I just wanted
To hear your voice
And to check if
You were alright
And to say
To you
Goodnight

I picked up my phone

I almost dialled
Your number
Then I remembered
You'd passed on
To the afterlife

I'll have to save
That conversation
For when
I see you
In the next life

I picked up my phone
To call you
Late last night

I almost dialled
Your number

Then I remembered

With Each Breath

Tonight it really does hurt
I see the sadness in his eyes
And the tears that well
When we share memories

I sat in your chair for a while
Remembering the lunchtimes
Where we sat and played cards
And we'd both drink tea

I remember you with each breath

It doesn't get easier
It just gets 'different'

I Call Him Freddy

I visited my Nanna Elliott
When I was but four

He was in the parlour
At the table
Dressed in black
Dark figure hunched over

I was on the sofa
Wrapped up home sick

We did not meet
As he sat so close
A thousand miles
Could have separated us

It appeared words were being had
Between he, my Sister and Nan
I have no recollection
Of this conversation

All I have is stories
Recalled by my siblings

I can not put pencil to page
To retell these tales
They have scarred me
Too deeply for words

For others memories
I have therapy

Twenty nine years
He's been dead for

Too disrespectful
It would be
To call him Dad

So how do I write
A poem about
That man
I never met?

Which Words Did You Write?

These questions I've often asked myself
Why though, as you were never in my life

What music did you like?
Which books did you read?
If you wrote poetry
Which I'm sure you did
Which words did you write?

A father, husband and lover
Brother, son and a soldier
A crippling mental health disorder
So along with the Schizophrenia
You probably suffered from
Post Traumatic Stress Disorder?

You were handy with your fists
You did like to set flight
Your black sack full of trophies
Thrown into the river Wear one night
You were good at this, right?

Your mum has been mentioned
On a couple of occasions
And I find this kind of odd
She did also like to fight

From the stories I've heard
Behind your blue eyes
Your mind it was, your mind was
As black as the darkest of nights

I'm not trying to justify your actions
Give your ashes excuses
From what I've been told
You were vile, violent and abusive

Was your demise justified
Some form of recompense
That you did choke to death
On your very own blood

There must have been some good
There must have been some love
I'd like to have just one hand shake
I'd like to have just one conversation

Questions and wondering why
As you were never in my life

What music did you like?
Which books did you read?
If you wrote poetry
Which I'm sure you did
Which words did you write?

"This was all the usual things..."

Sundays With The Boy

We eat a lot
We laugh a lot
We snuggle a lot
We play football a lot
We talk a lot
(About all sorts of stuff)

Did I mention that we eat a lot?
Did I mention we laugh a lot?
Did I mention we snuggle a lot?
Did I mention we play football a lot?
(Sometimes that's too much for my middle aged bones)
Did i mention we talk a lot?
(About all sorts of stuff)

I guess to sum things up
We do all this
But sometimes it is
Never enough

Our Routine

Two minutes and fifty seven seconds
Was the length of the telephone conversation
With my youngest son tonight

I ask him about his day
And he always asks me about mine

He did all the usual things in the morning
Which usually consists of
Literacy, numeracy and read-write-ink
With a healthy snack time thrown in

The afternoon was science
Measuring and recording information
Of the bean plants
The class have been growing

He talks about lunch
(He rarely remembers the details)
But pizza seems to be one of his favourite eatings
And of course at the age of seven
Playtime is his most favourite thing

Today he and his friends played Cheetahs
Which I'm told involves lots of running around
And hopefully not too much bumping into things

He goes from school to
After school club on a minibus
Although it's not far
Each day it's exciting

He plays with his friends
The activities depend on the weather

Today it rained
They played indoors
This was 'all the usual things'

They tidy up
They then have tea
His mum picks him
Up at five fifteen
And they go home
Except on Wednesdays
Because he has swimming

I know all this
Because we
He and me
Have our routine

I know I'm not there everyday
In a physical sense, but
I do what I can when I am
Which is every weekend

And each night
At 7pm
I call him

I ask him
About his day
And he always
Asks me about mine

PENCIL MARKS ON PAGES

A Tale Or Two

Every poet has a story to be told
Every poet has a story of the soul
Behind every pen stroke
Behind every observant eye
Is a puff of genius smoke

A long night spent writing
Creative expression
Delivering experience, a lesson
Every late night writing session
Bleary eyed
Dog tired and determined

The hours spent
On elbows lent
The tea drunk
Or the bourbon sunk
The screwed up paper pile
The electronic files
Saved for later

On elbows lent
The hours spent
Not easily pleased
Rarely satisfied
But ironically content

It's not all flowers
And windswept moors
Thatched cottages
And pink rose festooned porch

It's not all daffodils
And dry stone walls
Shakespearean tales
From a bygone age

It's more, it's more
Earthy than that
It kinda picks up
The track laid by
Ferlinghetti, Corso and Kerouac

Somewhat obviously that
I pointed those out
Any fool can list
Shit from Google
But a reader I'm not
I've just heard odds and sods

Soaking up influence
From the best wordsmiths
To grace this earth
I'll not list them
We've all got our favourites

But...
Every poet has a story
Every poet has a tale
So how about this
Let's share a few

After all
It's what we do

"Shifting perspective making changes…"

I Like It But It's Clunky

She said I like it but it's 'Clunky'
Well I'm not a bank of a thousand typewriting monkeys
Trying to be Shakespearian in a wordy old English fashion
I said it's more lumpy bumpy uneducated than clunky

No sonnet no Eliot Byron Betjeman
I'm not trying to preach with an amen
I'm trying to find it without too much fuss
And come it does battling dyslexic fuzz

The whir of hydraulic motor a constant mechanical buzz
Not the inspirational views over dale dry stone walled stuff
The words run around with no way out
Inside the house they shout
Window open a crack
Letting out

The constant up and down the stairs top to bottom
Knowing when you get there not what you've forgotten
In the kitchen of your mind back and forth rocking chair
Carbon monoxide inhalation oxygen starvation

Rattling key in back door lock
Hinge creaking open up step outside for a look

Blue skies, summer sun fresh air inspiration
Settled inside inspired at wordy progression

Pencil Marks On Pages

She's the type of girl who
Listens to Bach and Beethoven
And I'm the guy who just super glued
The cap from his tooth back on

I'm not saying it's a case of where you're from or social status
We talk and walk in different circles that's what became obvious
You see my day is spent drinking tea and writing poetry
No real direction or purpose, for now this may well be

I have plans to be making changes
I'm not talking about reworking world order
Nor do I have the ability to fix global conflicts and war

I've uttered these words before
I'm hatching plans

I'll chip away at it one day at a time
And not go down as one of history's greatest
But I'll leave a legacy that reaches out further
Than a positive update of a Facebook status

For my boys, my family
I show development in my wellbeing
And if this alone is my legacy
The positive pieces from this they are seeing

I'll not change the world with words
I'll make a difference to those who are my world
And for those who gain inspiration
From my unpunctuated ramblings
I thank you for listening
Life can be as bleak as
Listening to Parachutes by Coldplay

What are you saying, I'm listening
My door is open metaphorically speaking
If it's solace and a mug of tea you're seeking

Life changes, people places faces
Some remain the greatest
Others just life's detritus
Cut the strings and show forgiveness.

I'll continue to shift words and emotions
For me tea and poetry
Are my energising therapy

Books full of pencil marks on pages
Shifting perspective
Making changes

Self Educated Ramblings

I wandered lonely as a buttercup
And danced across moon filled sky
My head bobbed with the swaying of spring daffodils
And I fell in love with you
Under the dappled shade of the majestic oak tree

Seriously, clouds flowers and flouncy stuff
Well I really couldn't give a flying...

Flocks of geese and lambs born of sheep
Rolling moors, pink rose festooned porch
You'll know by now this isn't my beat
I'm more direct
Reflective selective about the words I spout

Black clouds and dark days
Wandering through life in a drug fuelled haze
Gaze vacant destructive implosive behaviour
Fighting sobriety trying to remain sober
Running through past times over and over

These amongst others are the subjects
That rattle around my grey matter

It's a riot of words ready to explode
Eroding your defenses
Battering down your fences
Provoking evoking memories

Words trapped under my skin
Like blisters
Waiting for a hot pin to be piercing

Tales of turmoil and trouble
Respectfully delivered with shivers
My skin tingles as words mingle
And resonate with listeners

I speak in 'lay terms'
Not impossible to understand verse
My lack of intellectual standing
Does not leave me face down

The words I deliver
Are self educated ramblings
No detangling needed
I just respectfully request
Your ears for listening

We all look up at the same sky
The same stars we all see at night
We speak in different tongues
All hearts speak the same language

Let's talk about this yeah?
Let's collectively share?

Because after all
It's about the words

I Wonder

Words flowing
Mind unknowing
Where this is going

I often wonder
As I lay awake
Where I'd be now

If I could
Erase
Mistakes?

"My skin tingles as words mingle..."

Wicker Not Wood

Just to make things clear
Just so you're hearing me

There was a point
Where I nearly disappeared me
To the point where
There would've been no more me

Throwing it all away as easily
As a food shopping list
Tossed away and dismissed
Without a second thinking
Thoughtlessly discarding
A life's worth of living
When I say living
My heart was just about beating

Always surrounded by those who had a plan
Which is drummed into you time and time again
Within the educational system and peer groups
And those oh so dear well meaning friends

Let me share with you this, after a moment of clarity
I'm a 47 year old man with a plan now before me
I'll not bore you or make you endure endless words
These ideas are becoming a solid reality

Life can be deceiving
A cluster-fuck of confusion
Disillusioned beyond belief
Grief stricken and choked
Fists gripped
Clenched teeth
Somehow still breathing
Without actually living

I will not fit inside a box
A shape and size of which is
Set out by this fucked up society
I will not just comply
I will no longer live
To be just living to die

As for that final box
I request wicker not wood
And my body six-foot deep
In a cemetery, buried
(I do not wish to be burned)

And on my headstone
That final statement
Should read

Here lays a Poet
Who lived

"It's what we do"